REJOICE!

REJOICE!

A Letter to Consecrated Men and Women

A Message from the Teachings of Pope Francis

Congregation for Institutes of Consecrated Life and Societies of Apostolic Life

Year of Consecrated Life

Paulist Press
New York / Mahwah, NJ

Cover design by Christina Cancel
Book design by Lynn Else

Library of Congress Cataloging-in-Publication Data

Catholic Church. Congregatio pro Institutis Vitae Consecratae et Societatibus Vitae Apostolicae.
    Rejoice! : a letter to consecrated men and women : a message from the teachings of Pope Francis / Congregation for Institutes of Consecrated Life and Societies of Apostolic Life, Year of Consecrated Life.
        pages cm
    Includes bibliographical references and index.
    ISBN 978-0-8091-4949-0 (pbk. : alk. paper) — ISBN 978-1-58768-561-3 (ebook : alk. paper)
    1. Joy—Religious aspects—Catholic Church. 2. Spiritual life—Catholic Church. I. Francis, Pope, 1936- II. Title.
    BX2350.3.C3823 2015
    248.8`94—dc23
                                                                    2015006841

ISBN 978-0-8091-4949-0 (paperback)
ISBN 978-1-58768-561-3 (e-book)

Published in the United States and Canada in 2015 by Paulist Press
997 Macarthur Boulevard
Mahwah, New Jersey 07430

www.paulistpress.com

Printed and bound in the
United States of America

"I want to say one word to you and this word is joy.

Wherever consecrated people are, there is always joy!"

Pope Francis

CONTENTS

DEAR BROTHERS AND SISTERS,

1. "The joy of the Gospel fills the heart and lives of all who encounter Jesus. With Jesus Christ joy is constantly born anew."[1]

The beginning of *Evangelii Gaudium*, within the fabric of the teaching of Pope Francis, rings out with surprising vitality, proclaiming the wonderful mystery of the Good News that transforms the life of the person who takes it to heart. We are told the parable of joy: our meeting with Jesus lights up in us its original beauty, the beauty of the face on which the Father's glory shines (cf. 2 Cor 4:6), radiating happiness.

This Congregation for Institutes of Consecrated Life and Societies of Apostolic Life invites us to reflect on the graced time we have been given to live, at the special invitation that the pope addresses to those in consecrated life.

To accept this teaching means to renew our existence in accordance with the Gospel, not in a radical way understood as a model of perfection and often of separation, but by adhering wholeheartedly to the saving encounter that transforms our life. "It is a question of leaving everything to follow the Lord. No, I do not want to say 'radical.' Evangelical radicalness is not only for religious: it is demanded of all. But religious follow the Lord in a special way, in a prophetic way. It is this witness that I expect of you. Religious should be men and women able to wake the world up."[2]

In their finite humanity, on the margins, in their everyday struggles, consecrated men and women live out their fidelity, giving a reason for the joy that lives in them. So they become splendid witnesses, effective proclaimers, companions and neighbors for the women and men with whom they share a common history and who want to find their Father's house in the Church.[3]

Francis of Assisi, who took the Gospel as his way of life "made faith grow and he renewed the Church, and at the same time he renewed society, he made it more fraternal, but he always did it with the Gospel and by his witness. Always preach the Gospel and if necessary use words!"[4]

Numerous suggestions come to us from listening to the words of the pope, but we are particularly challenged by the absolute simplicity with which Pope Francis offers his teaching, in tune with the appealing sincerity of the Gospel. Plain words sown from the open arms of the good sower, who trustingly does not discriminate between one sort of soil and another.

An authoritative invitation is offered to us with gentle trust, an invitation to do away with institutional arguments and personal justifications. It is a provocative word that questions our sometimes apathetic or sleepy way of life, as we often live on the margins of the challenge: *if you had faith as big as this mustard seed* (Luke 17:5). It is an invitation that encourages us to impel our spirits to acknowledge the Word living among us, the Spirit who creates and continues to renew the Church.

This Letter is motivated by this invitation, in the hope of initiating a shared reflection. It is offered as a simple tool for examining our lives honestly in the light of the Gospel. This Dicastery therefore presents a shared itinerary, a space for personal, communal, and institutional reflection as we journey toward 2015, the year the

Church has dedicated to consecrated life, with the desire and the intention of making courageous evangelical decisions leading to revitalization, bearing fruits of joy. "The primacy of God gives full meaning and joy to human lives, because men and women are made for God, and their hearts are restless until they rest in him."[5]

NOTES

1. Francis, Apostolic Exhortation *Evangelii Gaudium* (November 24, 2013), LEV, Vatican City, 2013, no. 1. All the cited texts of Pope Francis, with the exception of the morning meditations, are published in English on the Vatican Web site, http://w2.vatican.va/content /vatican/en.html.

2. Antonio Spadaro, "'Wake up the World!' Conversation with Pope Francis about the Religious Life," *La Civiltà Cattolica* 165 (2014/I): 5 (English translation by Fr. Donald Maldari, SJ).

3. Cf. Francis, *Evangelii Gaudium*, no. 47.

4. Francis of Assisi, *Meeting with the Young People of Umbria*, Assisi (Perugia), October 4, 2013.

5. John Paul II, Post-Synodal Apostolic Exhortation *Vita Consecrata* (March 25, 1996), no. 27, in: *AAS* 88 (1996): 377–486.

BE GLAD, REJOICE, RADIATE JOY

Rejoice with Jerusalem and be glad for her, all you who love her; rejoice greatly with her all you who mourn over her.

For this is what the Lord says: "I will extend peace to her like a river, and the wealth of nations like a flooding stream; you will nurse and be carried on her arm and dandled on her knees.

As a mother comforts her child, so will I comfort you; and you will be comforted over Jerusalem.

When you see this, your heart will rejoice and you will flourish like grass; the hand of the Lord will be made known to his servants."

Isaiah 66:10–14

LISTENING

2. In Sacred Scripture, the term *joy* (in Hebrew: *śimḥâ/śamaḥ, gyl*) is used to express a multiplicity of collective and personal experiences connected in a particular way to religious ceremonies and feasts, and to recognize the sense of the presence of God in the history of Israel. There are indeed thirteen different verbs and nouns found in the Bible to describe the joy of God, of people, and also of creation itself, in the dialogue of salvation.

In the Old Testament, these recurrences are most numerous in the Psalms and in the Prophet Isaiah. With creative and original linguistic variations, there are many invitations to joy. The joy of the nearness of God is proclaimed, the delight in what God has created and made. Hundreds of times in the Psalms there are effective expressions to indicate that joy is both the fruit of the benevolent presence of God and the jubilant echo that it gives rise to, as well as a declaration of the great promise that lies in the future for the people. As for the prophet, it is the second and third parts of the Book of Isaiah that pulse with this frequent call to joy, pointing to the future: it will be overflowing (cf. Isa 9:2), the heavens, the desert, and the earth will leap for joy (Isa 35:1; 44:23; 49:13), the liberated prisoners will enter Jerusalem shouting for joy (Isa 35:9ff.; 51:11).

In the New Testament, the preferred vocabulary is linked to the root *kar* (*kàirein, karà*), but other terms are found such as *agalliáomai, euphrosýnē*. It usually implies total exultation embracing the past and the future together. *Joy* is the messianic gift par excellence, as Jesus himself promised: *…that my joy may be in you and that your joy may be complete* (John 15:11; 16:24; 17:13). Starting with the events that precede the birth of the Savior, it is Luke who signals the exultant diffusion of joy (cf. Luke 1:14, 44, 47; 2:10; cf. Matt 2:10) and then accompanies the spread of the Good News with this effect that expands (cf. Luke 10:17; 24:41, 52) and is a typical sign of the presence and the spread of the Kingdom (cf. Luke 15:7, 10, 32; Acts 8:39; 11:23; 15:3; 16:34; cf. Rom 15:10–13; and so on).

According to Paul, joy is a fruit of the Spirit (cf. Gal 5:22) and a typical, constant feature of the Kingdom (cf. Rom 14:17) that is strengthened by trials and tribulations (cf. 1 Thess 1:6).

The source of joy must be found in prayer, charity, and unceasing thanksgiving (cf. 1 Thess 5:16; Phil 3:1; Col 1:11f.). In his difficulties the Apostle to the Gentiles felt full of joy and a sharer of the glory that we all await (cf. 2 Cor 6:10; 7:4; Col 1:24). The final triumph of God and the *marriage of the Lamb* will complete every joy and exultation (cf. Rev 19:7), setting off an explosion of a cosmic *Alleluia* (Rev 19:6).

Let us look at the meaning of the text: *Rejoice with Jerusalem and be glad for her, all you who love her; rejoice greatly with her* (Isa 66:10). This is the end of the third part of the Prophet Isaiah. It is necessary to be aware that chapters 65—66 are closely united and mutually complementary, as was already evident in the conclusion of the second part of Isaiah (chapters 54—55).

In both these chapters, the theme of the past is evoked, sometimes with crude imagery, as if to invite them to forget it because God wants to make a new light shine out, a trust that will immediately heal infidelity and cruelty. The curse, a result of their disregard for the Covenant, will disappear because God is about to make *Jerusalem a delight and its people a joy* (cf. Isa 65:18). This will be demonstrated in the experience that God's answer comes even before the request is voiced (cf. Isa 65:24). This context persists through the first verses of Isaiah 66, resurfacing here and there through signs showing the insensitivity of their hearts and ears in the face of the Lord's goodness and his Word of hope.

Here the likeness of Jerusalem as *mother* seems evocative. It is inspired by the promises of Isaiah 49:18–29 and 54:1–3: the land of Judah is unexpectedly filled with those returning from the diaspora, after their humiliation. You might almost say that the rumors of "liberation" had "made Zion pregnant" with new life and hope, and that God, the Lord of Life, will bring this pregnancy to fulfillment, effortlessly giving birth to new children. Thus mother Zion is surrounded by newborn children and generously nourishes and tends them all. This gentle image fascinated St. Thérèse of Lisieux, who found it a crucial key for the interpretation of her spirituality.[1]

An accumulation of intense words: *be glad, rejoice, radiate*, as well as *consolation, delight, abundance, prosperity, caresses*, and so on. The relationship of fidelity and love had failed, and they had ended in sadness and sterility. Now the power and holiness of God restores meaning and fullness of life and happiness, expressed in terms that belong to the affective roots of every human being, arousing unique feelings of tenderness and security.

It is a gentle but true profile of a God who radiates maternal vibrations and deep, contagious emotions. A heartfelt joy (cf. Isa 66:14) that comes from God—with maternal face and supportive arm—and radiates through a people who have been crippled, whose bones have become brittle through a thousand humiliations. It is a freely-given transformation that spreads out joyfully to the *new heavens and the new earth* (cf. Isa 66:22), so that all the people might come to know the glory of the Lord, the faithful redeemer.

JOY, THE BEAUTY OF CONSECRATION

3. "*This is the beauty of consecration: it is joy, joy....*"[2] The joy of bringing God's consolation to all. These are the words spoken by Pope Francis during his meeting with seminarians and novices. "There is no holiness in sadness,"[3]

the Holy Father continued. *Do not grieve like others who have no hope*, wrote St. Paul (1 Thess 4:13).

Joy is not a useless ornament. It is a necessity, the foundation of human life. In their daily struggles, every man and woman tries to attain joy and abide in it with the totality of their being.

In the world there is often a lack of joy. We are not called to accomplish epic feats or to proclaim high-sounding words, but to give witness to the joy that arises from the certainty of knowing we are loved, from the confidence that we are saved.

Our short memories and flimsy experiences often prevent us from searching for the "lands of joy" where we can relish God's reflection. We have a thousand reasons for remaining in joy. Its roots are nourished by listening with faith and perseverance to the Word of God. In the school of the Master we hear: *may my joy be in you and may your joy be complete* (John 15:11) and we are taught how to practice perfect joy. "Sadness and fear must give way to joy: *Rejoice…be glad…rejoice with her in joy*, says the prophet (Is 66:10). It is a great invitation to joy. […] Every Christian, and especially you and I, we are called to be bearers of this message of hope giving serenity and joy, God's consolation, his tenderness towards all. But if we first experience the joy of being consoled by him, of being loved by him, then we can bring that joy to others. […] I have occasionally met consecrated persons who are afraid of the consolations of God. They were tormented, because they were afraid of this divine tenderness. But be not afraid. Do not be afraid, because the Lord is the Lord of consolation, the Lord of tenderness. The Lord is a Father and he says that he will be for us like a mother with her baby, with a mother's tenderness. Do not be afraid of the consolations of the Lord."[4]

YOUR CALLING

4. "In calling you God says to you: 'You are important to me, I love you, I am counting on you'. Jesus says this to each one of us! Joy is born from that! The joy of the moment in which Jesus looked at me. Understanding and hearing this is the secret of our joy. Feeling loved by God, feeling

that for him we are not numbers but people; and we know that it is he who is calling us."[5]

Pope Francis directs our attention to the spiritual foundations of our humanity, to see what is given to us gratuitously by free divine sovereignty and free human response: *Then Jesus looked at him and loved him. "One thing you lack," he said. "Go, sell everything you have and give to the poor, and you will have treasure in heaven. Then come, follow me"* (Mark 10:21).

The pope recalls: "Jesus, at the Last Supper, turns to the Apostles with these words: *You did not choose me, but I chose you* (John 15:16). They remind us all, not only those of us who are priests, that vocation is always an initiative of God. It is Christ who called you to follow him in the consecrated life and this means continuously making an 'exodus' from yourselves in order to center your life on Christ and on his Gospel, on the will of God, laying aside your own plans, in order to say with St. Paul: *It is no longer I who live, but Christ who lives in me* (Gal 2:20)."[6]

The pope invites us on a *pilgrimage* in reverse, a pathway of knowledge to discover ourselves on the streets of Palestine or near the boat of the humble fisherman of Galilee. He invites us to contemplate the beginnings of a journey or rather, of an event initiated by Christ, when the nets were left on the lakeshore, the tax collector's desk by the side of the road, the ambitions of the zealot among discarded plans. All are inappropriate means for staying with him.

He invites us to remain for a long time, on an interior pilgrimage, before the dawn, when, in a warm environment of friendly relationships, the intellect is led to open itself to mystery, the decision is made that it is good to set out to follow this Master who alone has *the words of eternal life* (cf. John 6:68). He invites us to make our whole "life a pilgrimage of loving transformation."[7]

Pope Francis calls us to pause at that opening scene: "The joy of the moment when Jesus looked at me"[8] and to recall the important and demanding, underlying meaning of our vocation: "It is a response to a call, a call of love."[9] To stay with Christ requires us to share our lives, our choices, the obedience of faith, the happiness of poverty, the radicality of love.

It is about being reborn through vocation.

"I invite all Christians [...] at this very moment, to a renewed personal encounter with Jesus Christ today, at least to an openness to letting him encounter them; I ask all of you to do this unfailingly each day."[10]

Paul brings us back to this fundamental vision: *no one can lay any foundation other than the one already laid* (1 Cor 3:11). The word *vocation* indicates a free gift, like a reservoir of life that never ceases renewing humanity and the Church in the depths of their being.

In the experience of vocation, God is indeed the mysterious subject of an act of calling. We hear a voice that calls us to life and discipleship for the Kingdom. Pope Francis, in recalling "You are important to me," uses direct speech, in the first person, so that awareness might emerge. He calls to consciousness my opinion and my judgment, requiring behavior consistent with my self-awareness, with the call that I hear addressed to me, my personal call. "I would like to say to those who feel indifferent to God or to faith, and to those who are far from God or who have distanced themselves from him, and to us also, with our 'distancing' and our 'abandonment' of God, that may seem insignificant but are so numerous in our daily life: look into the depths of your heart, look into your own inner depths and ask yourself: do you have a heart that desires something great, or a heart that has been lulled to sleep by things? Has your heart maintained a restlessness searching or have you let it be suffocated by things that will finally harden it?"[11]

The relationship with Jesus Christ asks to be nourished by this restless searching. This makes us aware of the gratuity of the gift of a vocation and helps us to explain the reasons for our initial choice and for our perseverance. "Letting Christ make us his own always means straining forward to what lies ahead, to the goal of Christ (cf. Phil 3:14)."[12] To continue listening to God requires that these questions become the coordinates guiding the rhythm of our daily life.

This inexpressible mystery, leading us within, sharing in the indescribable mystery of God, can only be interpreted in faith. "Faith is our response to a word that engages us personally, to a 'Thou' who calls us by name"[13] and "as a response to a word which preceded it, would always be an act of remembrance. Yet this remembrance is not fixed on past events but, as the memory of a promise, it becomes capable of opening up the future, shedding light on the path to be taken."[14] "Faith contains our own memory of God's history with us, the memory of our encounter with God who always takes the first step, who creates, saves, and transforms us. Faith is remembrance of his word that warms our heart, and of his saving work which gives life, purifies us, cares for, and nourishes us. [...] The one who is mindful of God, who is guided by the memory of God in his or her entire life is able to awaken that memory in the hearts of others."[15] It is the memory of being called here and now.

FOUND, TOUCHED, TRANSFORMED

5. The pope asks us to reread our own personal story and to scrutinize it in the light of God's loving gaze, because if a vocation is always his initiative, it is up to us freely to accept the divine-human economy as a relationship of life in *agape*, the path of discipleship, the "beacon on the Church's journey."[16] Life in the Spirit is never completed, but is always open to mystery, as we discern in order to know the Lord and to

perceive reality beginning with him. When God calls us, he lets us enter into his rest and invites us to repose in him, in a continuous process of loving understanding. We hear the Word *you are worried and upset about many things* (Luke 10:41). On the path of love we go forward through rebirth: the old creation is born anew. *Therefore, if anyone is in Christ, that person is a new creation* (2 Cor 5:17).

Pope Francis points out the name of this rebirth. "This path has a name and a face: the face of Jesus Christ. He teaches us to become holy. In the Gospel, he shows us the way, the way of the Beatitudes (cf. Mt 5:1–12). This is the life of the Saints, people who for love of God did not place conditions on him during their life."[17]

Consecrated life is a call to incarnate the Good News, to *follow Christ*, the crucified and risen one, to take on "Jesus's way of living and acting as the Incarnate Word in relation to the Father and in relation to the brothers and sisters."[18] In practical terms, it is a call to take up his way of life, to adopt his interior attitude, to allow oneself to be invaded by his Spirit, to absorb his surprising logic and his scale of values, to share in his risks and his hopes. "Be guided by the humble yet joyful certainty of those who have been *found, touched and transformed by the Truth* who is Christ, ever to be proclaimed."[19]

Remaining in Christ allows us to grasp the presence of the Mystery which lives in us and expands our hearts to the measure of his Son's heart. Those who remain in his love, like the branch attached to the vine (cf. John 15:1–8), enter into intimacy with Christ and bear fruit. "Remain in Jesus! This means remaining attached to him, in him, with him, talking to him."[20]

"Christ is the seal on our foreheads, he is the seal on our hearts: on the forehead because we always profess him; on the heart because we always love him; he is the seal on our arms because we are always working for him."[21] Consecrated life is in fact a continuous call to follow Christ, and to be made like him. "Jesus's whole life, his way of dealing with the poor, his actions, his integrity, his simple daily generosity, and finally his complete self-giving, all this is precious and relates to our personal lives."[22]

Meeting the Lord gets us moving, urges us to leave aside self-absorption.[23] A relationship with the Lord is not static, nor is it focused on self. "Because when we put Christ at the center of our life, we ourselves don't become the center! The more that you unite yourself to Christ and he becomes the center of your life, the more he leads you out of yourself, leads you from making yourself the center and opens you to others."[24] "We are not at the center; we are, so to speak, 'relocated'. We are at the service of Christ and of the Church."[25]

Christian life is defined by verbs of movement. Even when it is lived in the context of a monastery or contemplative cloister, it is a life of continual searching.

"It is impossible to persevere in a fervent evangelization unless we are convinced from personal experience that it is not the same thing to have known Jesus as not to have known him, not the same thing to walk with him as to walk blindly, not the same thing to hear his word as not to know it, and not the same thing to contemplate him, to worship him, to find our peace in him, as not to do so. It is not the same thing to try to build the world with his Gospel as to try to do so by our own lights. We know well that with Jesus life becomes richer and that with him it is easier to find meaning in everything."[26]

Pope Francis recommends for us *restless searching* just like Augustine of Hippo: a "restlessness in his heart which brought him to a personal encounter with Christ, brought him to understand that the remote God he was seeking was the God who is close to every human being, the God close to our heart, who was more inward than our innermost self." This is an ongoing search. "Augustine did not stop, he did not give up, he did not withdraw into himself like those who have already arrived, but continued his search. The *restlessness of seeking the truth*, of seeking God, became restlessness to know him ever better and to come out of himself to make others know him. It was precisely the restlessness of love."[27]

JOY, A FAITHFUL "YES"

6. Anyone who has met the Lord and follows him faithfully is a messenger of the joy of the Spirit.

"Thanks solely to this encounter—or renewed encounter—with God's love, which blossoms into an enriching friendship, we are liberated from our narrowness and self-absorption."[28]

When we are called, we are called to our-selves, that is, to our capacity for being. Perhaps it is not unwarranted to say that the crisis of consecrated life results from the inability to rec-ognize such a profound call, even in those who are already living this vocation.

We are experiencing a crisis of fidelity, understood as a conscious adherence to a call that is a pathway, a journey from its mysterious beginnings to its mysterious end.

Perhaps we are also in a crisis of human-ization. We are experiencing the limitations of complete consistency, wounded by our incapac-ity to lead our lives as an integrated vocation and as a faithful journey.

This daily journey, both personal and com-munal, marked by discontent and a bitterness that encloses us in remorse, and almost in a per-manent longing for unexplored paths and unful-filled dreams, becomes a lonely road. Our call to live in relationship, in the fulfillment of love, can be transformed into an uninhabited wildness. At every age we are invited to revisit the deep center of our personal life, where the motivation of our life with the Master, as disciples of the Master, finds its meaning and truth.

Faithfulness is the awareness of a love that points us toward the "Thou" of God and toward every other person, in a constant and dynamic way when we experience within ourselves the life of the risen one. "Those who accept his offer of salvation are set free from sin, sorrow, inner emptiness, and loneliness."[29]

Faithful discipleship is grace and love in action; it is the practice of sacrificial charity. "When we journey without the Cross, when we build without the Cross, when we profess Christ without the Cross, we are not disciples of the Lord, we are worldly. We may be bishops, priests, cardinals, popes, but not disciples of the Lord."[30]

To persevere all the way to Golgotha, to experience the lacerations of doubts and denial, to rejoice in the marvel and wonder of the paschal event, up to the manifestation of Pentecost and the evangelization of the peoples, these are milestones of joyful fidelity because they are about self-emptying, experienced throughout life, even in the sign of martyrdom, and also sharing in the life of the risen Christ. "And it is from the Cross, the supreme act of mercy and love, that we are reborn as a *new creation*" (Gal 6:15).[31]

In the theological locus in which God, in revealing himself, reveals us to ourselves, the Lord asks us to return to the search, *fides quaerens. Pursue righteousness, faith, love and peace, along with those who call on the Lord out of a pure heart* (2 Tim 2:22).

The interior pilgrimage begins with prayer. "The first thing for a disciple is to be with the Master, to listen to him and to learn from him. This is always true, and it is true at every moment of our lives. […] If the warmth of God, of his love, of his tenderness is not in our own hearts, then how can we, who are poor sinners, warm the heart of others."[32] This is a lifelong journey, as in the humility of prayer, the Holy Spirit convinces us of the lordship of Christ within us. "The Lord calls us to follow him with courage and fidelity; he has made us the great gift of choosing us as his disciples; he invites us to proclaim him with joy as the Risen one, but he asks us to do so by word and by the witness of our lives, in daily life. The Lord is the only God of our lives, and he invites us to strip ourselves of our many idols and to worship him alone."[33]

The pope identifies prayer as the source of the fruitfulness of the mission. "Let us cultivate the contemplative dimension, even amid the whirlwind of more urgent and heavy duties. And the more the mission calls you to go out to the margins of existence, let your heart be the more closely united to Christ's heart, full of mercy and love."[34]

Being with Jesus shapes a contemplative approach to history which knows how to see and hear the presence of the Spirit everywhere and, in a special way, how to discern the Spirit's presence in order to live in time as God's time. When the insight of faith is lacking, "life itself loses meaning, the faces of brothers and sisters are obscured and it becomes impossible to recognize the face of God in them, historical events remain ambiguous and deprived of hope."[35]

Contemplation expands into prophetic aptitude. The prophet is one "whose eye is opened, and who hears and speaks the words of God; [...] a person of three times: the promise of the past, the contemplation of the present, the courage to point out the path toward the future."[36]

Fidelity in discipleship occurs through and is demonstrated by the experience of community, a theological reality in which we are called to support each other in our joyful "yes" to the Gospel. "It is the Word of God that inspires faith and nourishes and revitalizes it. And it is the Word of God that touches hearts, converting them to God and to his logic which is so different from our own. It is the Word of God that continually renews our communities."[37]

The pope invites us to renew our vocation and to fill it with joy and passion, so that the increase in loving activity is a continuous process—"it matures, matures, matures"[38]—in a permanent development in which the "yes" of our will to God's will unites will, intellect, and feeling. "Love is never finished and complete; throughout life it changes and matures, and thus remains faithful to itself."[39]

NOTES

1. With more references: cf. St. Thérèse of the Child Jesus, *Opere complete*, LEV–Ed. OCD, Vatican City–Rome, 1997: *Manoscritto A*, 76v°; B, 1r°; C, 3r°; *Lettera* 196.

2. Pope Francis, *Meeting with Seminarians and Novices*, Rome, July 6, 2013.

3. Ibid.

4. Pope Francis, *Homily for Holy Mass with Seminarians and Novices*, Rome, July 7, 2013.

5. Pope Francis, *Meeting with Seminarians and Novices*.

6. Pope Francis, *Address to the Participants at the Plenary Assembly of the International Union of Superiors General* (Rome, May 8, 2013), in: *AAS* 105 (2013): 460–63.

7. Pope Francis, *Message to the Prior General of the Order of Brothers of the Blessed Virgin Mary, on the Occasion of the General Chapter*, Rome, August 22, 2013.

8. Pope Francis, *Meeting with Seminarians and Novices*.

9. Ibid.

10. Pope Francis, *Evangelii Gaudium*, no. 3.

11. Pope Francis, *Homily for the Opening of the General Chapter of the Order of St. Augustine*, Rome, August 28, 2013.

12. Pope Francis, *Homily at the Holy Mass on the Feast of St. Ignatius Loyola*, Rome, July 31, 2013.

13. Pope Francis, Encyclical Letter *Lumen Fidei* (June 29, 2013), no. 8, in: *AAS* 105 (2013): 555–96.

14. Ibid., no. 9.

15. Pope Francis, *Homily at the Holy Mass for the Day for Catechists*, Rome, September 29, 2013.

16. Pope Francis, *Address to the Participants at the Plenary Assembly of the International Union of Superiors General*.

17. Pope Francis, *Angelus*, Rome, November 1, 2013.

18. John Paul II, Post-Synodal Apostolic Exhortation *Vita Consecrata* (March 25, 1996), no. 22, in: *AAS* 88 (1996): 377–486.

19. Pope Francis, *Homily at the Holy Mass with Bishops, Priests, Religious and Seminarians on the XXVIII World Youth Day*, Rio de Janeiro, July 27, 2013.

20. Pope Francis, *Address to the Participants at the International Congress on Catechesis*, Rome, September 27, 2013.

21. Ambrose, *De Isaac et Anima*, 75: PL 14, 556–57.

22. Pope Francis, *Evangelii Gaudium*, no. 265.

23. Cf. Pope Francis, *Evangelii Gaudium*, no. 265.

24. Pope Francis, *Address to the Participants at the International Congress on Catechesis*.

25. Pope Francis, *Homily at the Holy Mass on the Feast of St. Ignatius Loyola*.

26. Pope Francis, *Evangelii Gaudium*, no. 266.

27. Pope Francis, *Homily for the Opening of the General Chapter of the Order of St. Augustine*.

28. Pope Francis, *Evangelii Gaudium*, no. 8.

29. Ibid., no. 1.

30. Pope Francis, *Homily at the Holy Mass with the Cardinals* (Rome, March 14, 2013), in: *AAS* 105 (2013): 365–66.

31. Pope Francis, *Homily for Holy Mass with Seminarians and Novices.*

32. Pope Francis, *Address to the Participants at the International Congress on Catechesis.*

33. Pope Francis, *Homily at the Eucharistic Celebration at St. Paul Outside the Walls*, Rome, April 14, 2013.

34. Pope Francis, *Homily for Holy Mass with Seminarians and Novices.*

35. Congregation for Institutes of Consecrated Life and Societies of Apostolic Life, Instruction *Starting Afresh from Christ: A Renewed Commitment to Consecrated Life in the Third Millennium* (May 19, 2002), no. 25, in: *EnchVat* 21: 372–510.

36. Pope Francis, *Daily Meditation in the Chapel of* Domus Sanctae Marthae (December 16, 2013).

37. Pope Francis, *Meeting with the Clergy, Consecrated People and Members of Diocesan Councils*, Assisi (Perugia), October 4, 2013.

38. Pope Francis, *Meeting with Seminarians and Novices.*

39. Benedict XVI, Encyclical Letter *Deus Caritas Est* (December 25, 2005), no. 11, in: *AAS* 98 (2006): 217–52.

COMFORT, COMFORT MY PEOPLE

Comfort, comfort my people, says your God.

Speak tenderly to Jerusalem.

Isaiah 40:1–2

LISTENING

7. Using a stylistic peculiarity, also seen later in the text (cf. Isa 51:17; 52:1: *Awake, awake!*), the oracles of the second part of Isaiah (Isa 40—55) make a plea to come to the help of Israel in exile, shut up inside an empty memory of failure. The historical context clearly belongs to the prolonged exile of the people in Babylon (587–538 BC), with all the consequent humiliation and the sense of powerlessness to escape. However, the disintegration of the Assyrian empire under the pressure of the new emerging

power of the Persians, guided by the rising star of Cyrus, enabled the Prophet to foresee that an unexpected liberation might come about. And so it did. The Prophet, inspired by God, voiced this possibility publicly, interpreting the political and military developments as actions guided mysteriously by God through Cyrus. He proclaimed that liberation was at hand and that the return to the land of their fathers was about to take place.

The words that Isaiah uses: *Comfort...speak tenderly*, are found regularly in the Old Testament. These recurrences are of particular value in dialogues of tenderness and affection. Thus Ruth recognizes that Boaz has *"comforted me and spoken kindly"* (cf. Ruth 2:13), or in the famous page of Hosea who announces to the woman, Gomer, that he will "allure her and bring her into the wilderness and speak tenderly to her" (cf. Hos 2:16) for a new period of fidelity. There are other similar parallel passages: the dialogue of Shechem, son of Hamor, who was in love with Dinah (cf. Gen 34:1–5) and that of the Levite of Ephraim speaking to the concubine who had abandoned him (cf. Judg 19:3).

This is a language to be interpreted in the

context of love. Thus action and speech together, delicate and encouraging, remind us of the intense emotional bonds of God, the "spouse" of Israel. This *comfort* must be an epiphany of reciprocal belonging, an interplay of intense empathy, ferment, and vital connection. These are not superficial, cloying words, therefore, but mercy and deep-seated concern, an embrace giving strength and patient accompaniment in the rediscovery of faithful pathways.

BRINGING GOD'S EMBRACE

8. "People today certainly need words, but most of all they need us to bear witness to the mercy and tenderness of the Lord which warms the heart, rekindles hope, and attracts people towards the good. What a joy it is to bring God's consolation to others!"[1]

Pope Francis entrusts this mission to consecrated men and women: to discover the Lord who comforts us like a mother, and to comfort the people of God.

Service in the Church arises out of the joy of meeting the Lord and from his call. This mission is to bring to the men and women of our time the consolation of God, to bear witness to his mercy.[2]

In Jesus's view, consolation is a gift of the Spirit, the *Paraclete*, the Consoler who comforts us in our trials and awakes a hope that does not disappoint. Thus Christian consolation becomes comfort, encouragement, hope. It is the active presence of the Spirit (cf. John 14:16–17), the fruit of the Spirit. And *the fruit of the Spirit is love, joy, peace, patience, kindness, generosity, faithfulness, gentleness, and self-control* (Gal 5:22).

In a world of distrust, discouragement, and depression, in a culture in which men and women are enveloped by fragility and weakness, individualism and self-interest, we are asked to introduce belief in the possibility of true happiness, in the feasibility of hope that does not depend solely on talent, superiority, or knowledge, but on God. All are given the possibility of encountering him, if they only seek him with a sincere heart.

The men and women of our time are waiting for words of consolation, the availability of forgiveness and true joy. We are called to bring to everyone the embrace of God, who bends with a mother's tenderness over us—consecrated women and men, signs of the fullness of humanity, facilitators and not controllers of grace,[3] stooped down in a gesture of consolation.

TENDERNESS IS GOOD FOR US

9. Since we are witnesses of a communion beyond our vision and our limits, we are called to wear God's smile. Community is the first and most believable gospel that we can preach. We are asked to humanize our community. "Build friendship between yourselves, family life, love among you. May the monastery not be a Purgatory but a family. There are and there will be problems but like in a family, with love, search for a solution with love; do not destroy this to resolve that; do not enter competitions. Build community life, because in the life of a community it is this way, like a family, and it is the very Holy Spirit who is in the middle of the community. […] And community life always with a big heart. Let things go, do not brag, be patient with everything, smile from the heart. And a sign of this is joy."[4]

Joy is confirmed in the experience of community, that theological space where each one is responsible for their fidelity to the Gospel and for the growth of all. When a community is fed by the same Body and Blood of Jesus, it gathers around the Son of God, to share the journey of faith, guided by the Word. It becomes one with him, together in communion, experiencing the gift of love and festive celebration in freedom and joy, full of courage.

"A joyless community is one that is dying out. […] A community rich in joy is a genuine gift from above to brothers and sisters who know how to ask for it and to accept one another, committing themselves to community life, trusting in the action of the Spirit."[5]

In these days when fragmentation justifies widespread sterile individualism and when the weakness of relationships breaks up and ruins the care of the human person, we are invited to humanize community relationships, to encourage communion of heart and spirit in the Gospel sense, because "there is a communion of life among all those who belong to Christ. It is a communion that is born of faith" that makes "the Church, in her most profound truth, communion with God, intimacy with God, a communion of love with Christ and with the Father in the Holy Spirit, which extends to brotherly communion."[6]

For Pope Francis, the sign of fraternity is tenderness, a "Eucharistic tenderness" because "tenderness is good for us." Fraternity has "an enormous power to call people together. […] Fraternity, with all its possible diversity, is an experience of love which goes beyond conflicts."[7]

CLOSENESS AS COMPANIONSHIP

10. We are called to undertake an exodus out of our own selves, setting out on a path of adoration and service.[8] "We must go out through that door to seek and meet the people! Have the courage to go against the tide of this culture of efficiency, this culture of waste. Encountering and welcoming everyone, solidarity and fraternity: these are what make our society truly human. Be *servants of communion and of the culture of encounter*! I would like you to

be almost obsessed about this. Be so without being presumptuous."[9]

"The ghost to fight against is the image of religious life understood as an escape and consolation in face of an 'external' difficult and complex world."[10] The pope urges us to "leave the nest,"[11] to live the life of the men and women of our times, to hand ourselves over to God and to our neighbor.

"Joy is born from the gratuitousness of an encounter! [...] And the joy of the encounter with him and with his call does not lead to shutting oneself in but to opening oneself; it leads to service in the Church. St. Thomas said: *bonum est diffusivum sui*. Good spreads. And joy also spreads. Do not be afraid to show the joy of having answered the Lord's call, of having responded to his choice of love and of bearing witness to his Gospel in service to the Church. And joy, true joy, is contagious; it is infectious… it impels one forward."[12]

Faced with this contagious witness of joy, serenity, fruitfulness, the testimony of tenderness and love, humble charity, without arrogance, many people feel the need to "come and see."[13]

Many times Pope Francis has pointed out *the path of attraction*, of contagion, the path for the growth of the Church, the path of the new evangelization. "The Church must be attractive. Wake up the world! Be witnesses of a different way of acting, of living! It is possible to live differently in this world. [...] It is this witness I expect from you."[14]

Entrusting to us the task of *waking up the world*, the pope urges us to approach the stories of the men and women of today in the light of two pastoral categories that have their roots in the newness of the Gospel: *closeness* and *encounter*, two ways through which God himself is revealed in history culminating in the Incarnation.

On the road to Emmaus, like Jesus with his disciples, we welcome in daily companionship the joys and sorrows of the people, giving them "heart warmth,"[15] while we tenderly care for the tired and the weak, so that our journey together has light and meaning in Christ.

Our journey together "matures towards pastoral fatherhood, towards pastoral motherhood, and when a priest is not a father to his community, when a sister is not a mother to all those with whom she works, he or she becomes sad. This is the problem. For this reason I say to you: the root of sadness in pastoral life is precisely in the absence of fatherhood or motherhood that comes from living this consecration unsatisfactorily, which on the contrary should lead us to fertility."[16]

THE RESTLESSNESS OF LOVE

11. As living icons of the motherhood and of the closeness of the Church, we go out to those who are waiting for the Word of consolation and we bend down with motherly love and fatherly spirit toward the poor and the weak.

The pope invites us *not to privatize love*, but with the restlessness of the seeker: "Tirelessly seeking the good of the other, of the beloved."[17]

The crisis of meaning of the modern person and the economic and moral crisis of western society and its institutions are not temporary phenomena of the times in which we live but they outline an historical moment of outstanding importance. We are called now, as the Church, to go outside in order to arrive at the margins, geographic, urban, and existential—the margins of the mystery of sin, pain, injustice, and misery—to the hidden places of the soul where each person experiences the joys and sufferings of life.[18]

"We live in a culture of conflict, a culture of fragmentation, a culture of waste [...]. The discovery of a tramp who has died of cold is not news." Yet poverty for us is a theological category, "because our God, the Son of God, abased himself, he made himself poor to walk along the road with us. [...] A poor Church for the poor begins by reaching out to the flesh of Christ. If we reach out to the flesh of Christ, we begin to understand something, to understand what this poverty, the Lord's poverty, actually is."[19] To experience in one's own life the beatitude of the poor means to be a sign that the anguish of loneliness and limitation has been conquered by the joy of the person who is indeed free in Christ and has learned how to love.

During his pastoral visit to Assisi, Pope Francis was asked what the Church must strip away. And he replied: "[Strip away] every action that is not for God, is not of God; strip away the fear of opening the doors and going out to encounter all, especially the poorest of the poor, the needy, the remote, without waiting. Certainly not to get lost in the shipwreck of the world, but to bear with courage the light of Christ, the light of the Gospel, even in the darkness, where one can't see, where one might stumble. Strip away the seeming assurance structures give, which, though certainly necessary and important, should never obscure the one true strength it carries within: God. He is our strength!"[20]

This resonates like an invitation for us "not to be afraid of the newness the Holy Spirit works within us, not to be afraid of the renewal of structures. The Church is free. She is sustained by the Holy Spirit. It is this that Jesus teaches us in the Gospel: the freedom we need always to find the newness of the Gospel in our life and in structures, the freedom to choose new wineskins for this newness."[21] We are invited to be audacious, frontier men and women: "Ours is not a 'lab faith,' but a 'journey faith,' an historical faith. God has revealed himself as history, not as a compendium of abstract truths. [...] You cannot bring home the frontier, but you have to live on the border and be audacious."[22]

Besides the challenge of the beatitude of

the poor, the pope invites us to visit the frontiers of thought and culture, to promote dialogue, even at the intellectual level, to give reasons for hope on the basis of ethical and spiritual criteria, questioning ourselves about what is good. Faith never restricts the space for reason, but opens it to a holistic vision of the human person and of reality, and defends it against the danger of reducing the human person to "human material."[23]

Authentic culture, constantly called to serve humanity in all its conditions, opens unexplored paths, opens doors to allow hope to breathe, strengthens the meaning of life, and watches over the common good. An authentic cultural process "promotes an integral humanism and the culture of encounter and relationship: this is the Christian way of promoting the common good, the joy of living. Here, faith and reason unite, the religious dimension and the various aspects of human culture—art, science, labor, literature…."[24] Authentic cultural research encounters history and opens up ways of seeking the face of God.

The places where knowledge is developed and communicated are also the places where a culture of closeness, of encounter and dialogue, can be created that lowers defenses, opens doors, and builds bridges.[25]

NOTES

1. Pope Francis, *Homily for Holy Mass with Seminarians and Novices.*

2. Cf. Pope Francis, *Meeting with Seminarians and Novices.*

3. Cf. Pope Francis, *Evangelii Gaudium*, no. 47.

4. Pope Francis, *Address to the Cloistered Nuns*, Assisi (Perugia), October 4, 2013.

5. Congregation for Institutes of Consecrated Life and Societies of Apostolic Life, Instruction *Fraternal Life in Community. "Congregavit nos in unum Christi amor"* (February 2, 1994), no. 28: in *EnchVat* 14: 345–537.

6. Pope Francis, *General Audience*, Rome, October 30, 2013.

7. Spadaro, "'Wake up the World!'" 13.

8. Cf. Pope Francis, *Address to the Participants at the Plenary Assembly of the International Union of Superiors General.*

9. Pope Francis, *Homily at the Holy Mass with Bishops, Priests, Religious and Seminarians on the XXVIII World Youth Day.*

10. Spadaro, "'Wake up the World!'" 10.

11. Cf. ibid., 6.

12. Pope Francis, *Meeting with Seminarians and Novices.*

13. Cf. Pope Francis, *Morning Meditation in the Chapel of* Domus Sanctae Marthae.

14. Spadaro, "'Wake up the World!'" 5.

15. Cf. Pope Francis, *Meeting with the Brazilian Bishops*, Rio de Janeiro, July 24, 2013.

16. Pope Francis, *Meeting with Seminarians and Novices.*

17. Pope Francis, *Homily for the Opening of the General Chapter of the Order of St. Augustine.*

18. Cf. Pope Francis, *Vigil of Pentecost with the Movements, New Communities, Associations and Lay Groups* (Rome, May 18, 2013), in: *AAS* 105 (2013): 450–52.

19. Ibid.

20. Pope Francis, *Meeting with the Poor Assisted by Caritas*, Assisi (Perugia), October 4, 2013.

21. Pope Francis, *Morning Meditation in the Chapel of* Domus Sanctae Marthae.

22. Antonio Spadaro, Interview with Pope Francis, *La Civiltà Cattolica* 164 (2013/III): 474.

23. Cf. Pope Francis, *Meeting with the World of Culture*, Cagliari, September 22, 2013.

24. Pope Francis, *Meeting with the Brazilian Leaders*, Rio de Janeiro, July 27, 2013.

25. Cf. Pope Francis, *Address to the Community of Writers of "La Civiltà Cattolica,"* Rome, June 14, 2013.

FOR REFLECTION

12. As a global network in which we are all connected, where no local tradition can aspire to a monopoly of the truth, where technologies affect everyone, the world throws down a continuous challenge to the Gospel and to those who shape their lives in accordance with the Gospel.

In this historical process, through choices and ways of living, Pope Francis is building up a living hermeneutic of the dialogue between God and the world. We are introduced to a style of wisdom rooted in the Gospel and in human eschatology, which interprets pluralism, searches for equilibrium, invites us to facilitate the capacity of being responsible for change so that the truth of the Gospel might be better communicated, while we move "within the limits of language and of circumstances."[1] Aware of these limits, each one of us becomes *weak with the weak…all things to all people* (1 Cor 9:22).

We are invited to promote a generative, not simply administrative, dynamic to embrace the spiritual events present in our communities and in the world, movements and grace that the Spirit works in each individual person, viewed as a person. We are invited to commit ourselves to dismantling lifeless models, to describing the human person as marked by Christ, who is never revealed absolutely in speech or actions.

Pope Francis invites us to a wisdom that should be demonstrated by flexible consistency, the ability of consecrated people to respond in accord with the Gospel, to act and to choose in accord with the Gospel, without losing ourselves among the different spheres of life, language, or relationships, maintaining an awareness of responsibility, of the networks that bind us together, of the finitude of our limits, of the infinite number of ways in which life is expressed. A missionary heart is a heart that has known the joy of Christ's salvation and shares it as consolation: "[This heart] realizes that it has to grow in its own understanding of the Gospel and in discerning the paths of the Spirit, and so it always does what good it can, even if in the process, its shoes get soiled by the mud of the street."[2]

Let us welcome the encouragement that the pope offers us to see ourselves and the world with the eyes of Christ and to remain concerned about it.

QUESTIONS FROM POPE FRANCIS

- I want to say one word to you and this word is *joy*. Wherever there are consecrated people, seminarians, men and women religious, young people, there is joy, there is always joy! It is the joy of freshness, the joy of following Jesus; the joy that the Holy Spirit gives us, not the joy of the world. There is joy! but—where is joy born?[3]

- Look into the depths of your heart, look into your own inner depths and ask yourself: Do you have a heart that desires something great, or a heart that has been lulled to sleep by things? Has your heart preserved the restlessness of seeking or have you let it be suffocated by things that end by hardening it? God awaits you, he seeks you; how do you respond to him? Are you aware of the situation of your soul? Or have you nodded off? Do you believe God is waiting for you or does this truth consist only of "words"?[4]

- We are victims of this culture of the temporary. I would like you to think about this: How can I be free, how can I break free from this "culture of the temporary"?[5]

- This is a primary responsibility of all adults, of formators: to set an example of consistency to the youngest. Do we want consistent young people? Are we consistent? On the contrary, the Lord will say to us what he said to the People of God about the Pharisees: "Do what they say but not what they do!" Consistency and authenticity![6]

- We may ask ourselves: Am I anxious for God, anxious to proclaim him, to make him known? Or do I allow that spiritual worldliness to attract me which impels people to do everything for love of themselves? We consecrated people think of our personal interests, of the functionality of our works, of our careers. Well, we can think of so many things....Have I, so to speak, made myself "comfortable" in my Christian life, in my priestly life, in my religious life, and also in my community life? Or do I retain the force of restlessness for God, for his Word that makes me "step out" of myself towards others?[7]

- Do we feel the restlessness of love? Do we believe in love for God and for others? Or are we unconcerned by this? Not in an abstract manner, not only in words, but the real brother we come across, the sister who is beside us! Are we moved by their needs or do we remain closed in on ourselves, in our communities which are often "comfortable communities" for us?[8]

- This is a beautiful, beautiful way to holiness! Do not speak badly of others. "But father, there are problems...." Tell the superior, tell the Bishop, who can rectify them. Do not tell a person who cannot help. This is important: brotherhood! But tell me, would you speak badly of your mother, your father, your siblings? Never. So why do you do so in the consecrated life, in the seminary, in your priestly life? Only this: think, think.... Brotherhood! This brotherly love.[9]

- At the foot of the Cross, Mary is at the same time the woman of sorrow and of watchful expectation of a mystery far greater than sorrow, which is about to be fulfilled. It seemed that everything had come to an end; every hope could be said to have been extinguished. She too, at that moment, remembering the promises of the Annunciation could have said: they did not come true, I was deceived. But she did not say this. And so she who was blessed because she believed, sees blossom from her faith a new future and awaits God's tomorrow with expectation. At times I think: do we know how to wait for God's tomorrow? Or do we want it today? For her, the tomorrow of God is the dawn of Easter morning, the dawn of the first day of the week. It would do us good to think, in contemplation, of the embrace of mother and son. The single lamp lit at the tomb of Jesus is the hope of the mother, which in that moment is the hope of all humanity. I ask myself and I ask you: Is this lamp still alight in monasteries? In your monasteries are you waiting for God's tomorrow?[10]

- The restlessness of love is always an incentive to go towards the other, without waiting for the other to manifest his need. The restlessness of love gives us the gift of pastoral fruitfulness, and we must ask ourselves, each one of us: is my spiritual effectiveness healthy, is my apostolate fruitful?[11]

- An authentic faith always involves a profound desire to change the world. Here is the question we must ask ourselves: Do we also have great vision and impetus? Are we also daring? Do our dreams fly high? Does zeal consume us (cf. Ps 68:10)? Or are we mediocre and satisfied with our "made in the lab" apostolic programs?[12]

NOTES

1. Pope Francis, *Evangelii Gaudium*, no. 45.

2. Ibid.

3. Pope Francis, *Meeting with Seminarians and Novices*.

4. Pope Francis, *Homily for the Opening of the General Chapter of the Order of St. Augustine*.

5. Pope Francis, *Meeting with Seminarians and Novices*.

6. Ibid.

7. Pope Francis, *Homily for the Opening of the General Chapter of the Order of St. Augustine*.

8. Ibid.

9. Pope Francis, *Meeting with Seminarians and Novices*.

10. Pope Francis, *Celebration of Vespers with the Community of Camaldolese Benedictine Nuns*, Rome, November 21, 2013.

11. Pope Francis, *Homily for the Opening of the General Chapter of the Order of St. Augustine*.

12. Pope Francis, *Homily at the Holy Mass in the Church of the Gesù on the Feast of the Holy Name of Jesus*, Rome, January 3, 2014.

HAIL, MOTHER OF JOY

13. *Rejoice, full of grace* (Luke 1:28), "the greeting of the angel to Mary is an invitation to joy, to a deep joy, announcing the end of sadness....It is a greeting that marks the beginning of the Gospel, the Good News."[1]

Alongside Mary joy expands. The Son she carries in her womb is the God of joy, of contagious, engaging delight. Mary throws open the doors of her heart and runs to Elizabeth.

"Joyful in achieving her desires, sensitive in her duty, thoughtful in her joy, she hurries towards the mountain. Where, if not towards the summit, should she set out so kindly, she who was already full of God?"[2]

She went *in great haste* (Luke 1:39) to bring the happy news to the world, to bring all the uncontainable joy she held in her womb: Jesus, the Lord. *In great haste*: it is not only the speed with which Mary went. We are told of her diligence, the careful attention with which she undertakes the journey, her enthusiasm.

Behold the servant of the Lord (Luke 1:38). The Lord's servant ran *in great haste*, to become the servant of all people.

In Mary the Church is all who journey together: in the love of those who go out to the most fragile; in the hope of those who know that they will be accompanied in their going out and in the faith of those who have a special gift to share. In Mary each one of us, driven by the wind of the Spirit, fulfills our own vocation to move out!

> Star of the new evangelization,
> help us to bear radiant
> witness to communion,
> service, ardent and generous faith,
> justice and love of the poor,
> that the joy of the Gospel
> may reach to the ends of the earth,
> illuminating even the fringes of the world.
> Mother of the living Gospel,
> wellspring of happiness for God's little ones,
> Pray for us.
> Amen. Alleluia![3]

Rome, February 2, 2014
Feast of the Presentation of the Lord
João Braz Card. de Aviz
Prefect

† José Rodríguez Carballo, O.F.M.
Archbishop Secretary

NOTES

1. Benedict XVI, *General Audience*, Rome, December 19, 2012.

2. Ambrose, *Expositio Evangelii Secundum Lucam*, II, 19: CCL 14, p. 39.

3. Pope Francis, *Evangelii Gaudium*, no. 288.